T0077993

MIND *Your* BUSINESS

E . K I N N A R D M O S S

authorHOUSE

AuthorHouse™
1663 Liberty Drive
Bloomington, IN 47403
www.authorhouse.com
Phone: 833-262-8899

Published by AuthorHouse 06/07/2022

ISBN: 978-1-6655-4638-6 (sc)
ISBN: 978-1-6655-4637-9 (e)

Library of Congress Control Number: 2021924521

Print information available on the last page.

CONTENTS

INTRODUCTION

Time is valuable and purpose fulfilled is rewarding. Don't bury your talent; live your life to its full potential. Fear can be your number-one enemy, but with hard work and determination, you can reach that dream. What you do today determines your future. Nothing happens overnight, so patience and endurance are must haves when you are trying to become successful. Think positive thoughts, and use your time and energy wisely as positive energy activates constant elevation. The world belongs to the optimistic; nothing good comes from negativity. Continue to build, and one day you will feel the thrill of victory, not the agony of defeat. Channel your energy in the right direction, and you will continue to make progress. Analyze life in a respectable mindset and be great.

Once you accomplish all that you have set out to do, you achieve immortality. Your greatness will forever be spoken of. Be all that you can be, and you will inspire others to do the same. There's always somebody watching you. Be accountable for your choices, and never doubt your abilities. Not everyone will be proud of you, but they will wonder how you make it happen. Success is the greatest middle finger of all. Become the best version of yourself, and to hell with the rest.

DEDICATION

In honor of my father, Mr. Donald Moss.

You instilled in me so much. You were the first person who said to me, "Boy, everything you touch turns into gold." I have always admired you for your business mind. While growing up, I watched you begin three businesses. Because of you I went to plenty of professional football, basketball, and baseball games. You taught me business and how to invest in myself. You challenged me to be creative and to find out what I liked to do. You never cared what people thought of you. You just did you. You taught me to look like money even if I was broke. You taught me that one thing always leads to another. You taught me to dance with my woman and to be a family man. You taught me what it is to be a man. You taught me what is important in life and what isn't. Because of you I am a man, a businessman. You are my Superman. I honor, respect, and love you, man.

CHAPTER 1

THE TASK AT HAND

STARVE YOUR DISTRACTION, AND FEED your focus. In order for you to do big things in life, you must be willing to sleep outside and come out from your comfort zone. A comfort zone is a beautiful place, but nothing ever grows there. You can either work nine to five your entire life or bring forth your own ideas. If you are passionate about something, then that is what you are supposed to be doing. And with hard work and determination, you can make it come to pass. You must be willing to sacrifice unless you have a lot of money. Everything takes money, and I don't think it's going to happen overnight. After all, Rome wasn't built in a day (or night). It's always good to have support and someone who believes in you, but it's your vision, and everybody wasn't meant to see things like you do. It's up to you to be true to yourself and believe in what you are doing. Be confident and know without a shadow of a doubt that you can bring your vision to pass. Write the vision down on paper and make it plain so you will chase after it.

Anything worth having is worth working for. You will surely face obstacles, so have a little faith. But faith alone is not going to do it. Faith without works is dead. Business is not for everyone. If this is something you can see yourself doing, then it's for you. If you can see yourself being a boss, then you can be one. You must be self-motivated and focused on what's important. You must use your time wisely. You're not going to make it to the family reunion or a night out on the town with your homies because you have work to be done.

Remember, it takes money to make money, so you can't afford to be wasteful. It takes constant investment in order to run a business. Just because you have money doesn't mean you can spend it. Don't think that someone is going to give you anything because you are doing something good. People don't care if you succeed or not. Some hope that you don't. Try not to deal with your family or friends until you have completed what you have set out to do. Some will try and make you feel like what you are doing is not important. To them it's not. People have their own lives, and so do you. There will be times that you wish you could do more. Don't beat yourself up; just keep on building. Be proud of yourself and what you have accomplished thus far.

If one door closes, knock on the back door. It's all about information, and there are different ways of doing things. Research is a must when trying to start a business. One company may tell you how much exposure it can bring to your business and charge you an arm and a leg for it, while you can do it for yourself. When starting out, it's good to find the cheapest way out. Always set short-term and long-range goals. Having a budget is mandatory and an extra way to make money. You will have your everyday life expenses plus what you're trying to pursue. There may come times when you have to go without lights or eating at a fine restaurant. If you don't budget your finances well, you could even end up homeless. The question is, "How bad do you want it?"

Your spouse must believe in you and be willing to suffer the hard times because they may surely come. "If you dare to struggle, you dare to win. If you dare not to struggle, then damn it you don't deserve to win" (Fred Hampton). As long as you're both headed in the same direction, the road is easier to travel. Be honest with yourself and have dignity in your business. When people respect you, they will be inclined to believe in you and do business with you. You want to have faithful customers, and people who will recommend your business to others. Be willing to give away free stuff. By doing that you show people that they're dealing with someone who is genuine. If they can get good free stuff from you, they're more likely to keep coming back and spending money with you.

Keep your audience intrigued. Believe in yourself, and others will believe in you. People make the world go around, and your audience is your most important asset. Never stop thinking of ways to make them want your product or services. See your art, read your words, or hear your voice. If what you have is good, they will buy into your ideas. If you build it, they will come. Treat everyone with the same amount of respect. In business you don't see race or color. Barry Gordy said all he seen was the color green.

Be open to suggestions. Put yourself in the right places. You are just starting out, and entrepreneurs who have been in business much longer know way more than you can ever imagine. Stay humble. Just because you're taking a chance does not mean it's going to work. Remember, it's a leap of faith that you decided to take. This is something you have never done before. Nobody knows what tomorrow may bring.

On your way up, life doesn't stop. You will have funerals to attend, cars that need repairing, children to attend to, and bills to be paid. You cannot afford to get the big head. Life brings all sorts of distractions, so remind yourself to mind your business. Time waits for no one, so stay focused, and you will accomplish your goals. It's easy to waste time and do nothing. Success is work, but to achieve your ideas is golden.

CHAPTER 2

BLACK ENTREPRENEURSHIP

BLACK ENTREPRENEURSHIP IS BIG BUSINESS and getting a lot of attention. Since the pandemic, there has been a rise in black-owned businesses.

Time has always been an issue. When most of your day is spent working, there is never enough time to invest in yourself. Now is the time to bring forth your ideas that have been lying dormant for so long. On average 380 out of every 100,000 Black adults became new entrepreneurs during the 2020 pandemic, up from 240 in each of the prior two years, according to a study based on census data. Small Black-owned businesses make up a crucial part of the small business economy.

We have dealt with many obstacles to become business owners. Now we want to be our own bosses. We face the normal challenges of running a business, not to mention the funding gap between Black and White America. Eight out of ten Black-owned businesses fail within the first eighteen months. Since COVID-19, just as you see Black ownership on the rise, other small Black-owned businesses were impacted tremendously. Some closed, never to reopen. There is a need and there must be an interest in supporting the economic advancement of African Americans.

For the first time, some businesses received government help in the form of a Paycheck Protection Program (PPP) loan. Others did not take advantage of the program because it was foreign to them. We definitely all make for a good underdog story. We want more success stories. We want to be able to sustain that which we have started. To build and add on is the goal. We seek to provide job opportunities and inspire our next generation to become business owners.

At the same time, we must support Black-owned businesses; that's how you build generational wealth. The Black population has much purchasing power. It also influences mainstream society—what Black people do becomes trendy. Everybody wants to be like us but don't want to be us. The Black population is a multibillion-dollar industry all on its own. The same way we stimulate the US economy, we must stimulate businesses in our own communities. Our spending habits are making everybody rich but us.

In a capitalist society, you have two kinds of people: the consumer and the seller. Either you're selling or you're buying. This is commerce. We must take advantage of the resources that we have available. We must make the right investments and utilize any loans or grants in the correct manner. We must strategize to win and cut back on unnecessary spending.

We must educate ourselves better when it comes to business and finance. We miss out on a lot of opportunities due to lack of knowledge. A lot of our people attend college and, once they graduate, don't work in the profession they went to school for. We need more business mindsets in Black communities. We need the right education and the right information.

It's our time to get off this treadmill of life and boss up. We have a history of creating something out of nothing. Be willing to fail while you're on the road to entrepreneurship. The only thing on the other side of failure is success. It's in you to do it, but most won't try because they fear failure. We need business development in the Black community. We need people who will help critique the ideas of our upcoming business owners and entrepreneurs. Until these resources become available, we must be relentless in research and exploration.

We need mentorship about how to access capital and how to break the barriers Black entrepreneurs experience. You can make it happen with the right information and the right education. It's disturbing once you find out that you don't need a college degree to start your own business, but you do need a degree to work for a successful firm or gain a title at some successful corporation.

Let's be smart with our time and energy. If you're going to labor, you might as well labor for yourself. Be a part of the "Black business on the rise" movement. Surround yourself with people who are moving in the same direction and have the same mindset that you do. There's a great number of Black business owners, but it's the next level we must reach. We must break that barrier and create jobs for ourselves. Out of the two million Black businesses, only 107,000 of them have employees other than the owner. Having access to people smarter than you are is a blessing, not a threat. We need a coalition of Black business owners who are ready to take their businesses to the next level. The

Black unemployment rate has been going up because employers are still passing over Black workers.

There is an opportunity gap. Most Black households earn, on average, little more than half of what the average White households earn. White households are, on average, thirteen times wealthier than Black households. If we need more college graduates, then so be it, but to be part of the solution, we must create jobs. Let's not continue to be dependent on another race to do for us what we can do for ourselves. If you want to leave your children an inheritance, how about a limited liability corporation (LLC)? It's up to us to change our situation and our future.

You are an intelligent race of people who are already equipped with knowledge to move forward. We must stop denying our greatness and be who God has called us to be. We control our own destiny. We have been standing in line for a slice of America's pie for far too long. Their feet have been on our necks. The only way to close a wealth gap is with wealth. So market your brand and take a chance on yourself and your ideas.

We need more entrepreneurs. We need those in the so-called 1 percent to mentor upcoming business owners and show them how to succeed. There are men and women who have built empires across industries, inspired millions, and supported the next generation of Black founders striving to make it big. Very few of us are among that wealthiest 1 percent. A lot has to do with generational wealth built on slave labor. We have a long way to go in order to catch up. We have the education, but we must apply ourselves in different areas of life. If we only think of ourselves and our own households, our future will be lacking and so will the nation in general.

If you have a nursing degree, instead of just being the head nurse at somebody else's establishment, open your own medical facility. If you're a teacher, open a school and teach others what you know. Maybe your students will open their own establishments.

We must create jobs and build wealth in the Black community. Let's build Black economic wealth and be self-sufficient like we once were in Tulsa and Rosewood. Once we accept the fact that the Black community is on its own and we're all in this together, the quicker we will stand up and be that mighty nation of people that we are. Being the best version of yourself means not working for somebody else for your entire life. You have creative minds and are capable of seeing your visions come to pass.

Let's normalize entrepreneurship conversations in the home.

> Success isn't about how much money you make, its about the difference you make in people's lives.
>
> —Michelle Obama

Leave a blueprint for your children to follow. You always need a plan B, and you don't need a degree to obtain a business license.

God created you to be the head and not the tail.

You have been at the bottom of the social totem pole for far too long. Think outside the box. Use your mind, time, and energy to create your own box. Find out what it is that you're passionate about and market your brand. If Ralph Lauren can come up with quality designs that we so much love and admire, then so can you. If you want to open your own school and teach your children business and finance in the sixth grade, you very well can. We must stop underestimating ourselves and be who we know we are.

What is it all worth? You're creating a pathway for your future. Your children will not live their lives to their full potential unless you do. If you just skate by, so will they. Don't let the cares of life steal your ambitions. Get up, dress up, show up, and show out. Go the extra mile—it's never crowded there. Stay positive, work hard, and make it happen. Exercising the will to set up a business is a way to freedom. Doing something for ourselves is the way to gain respect and recognition as a people. Stop looking at things as if those things are gonna change. No matter what your beliefs are, nothing is going to change unless you change your mindset. Life is about evolving.

Don't stay in a situation that's not helping you grow. Replace your doubts with confidence. Whatever you're willing to put up with is exactly what you will have. You will never be all that God intended for you to be if you work for someone else for your entire life.

> And God blessed them, and God said unto them, Be fruitful, and multiply, and replenish the earth, and subdue it: and have dominion over the fish of the sea, and over the fowl of the air, and over every living thing that moveth upon the earth.
>
> —Genesis 1:28

We weren't created to settle for less. We were created to conquer and subdue. We were not created to lack and not have. Information is at our fingertips. You can have what the next man has. The internet has fundamentally changed everything. Previously, knowledge was locked away in the minds of industry experts and in the pages of books that you needed to buy or check out from a library. But now, it's easier than ever to learn new skills. This is essential to becoming the best version of yourself.

Having something you love to do outside of work helps you to become the best version of yourself. If it's productive, it just might become your full-time job. You empower yourself by the actions you take for you and the generations to come. Opportunity is missed by most people because it is dressed in overalls and looks like work.

Parents are a child's first role models and influences. If you excel in life, your children will not settle for a life of mediocrity. They will not settle for a world in which the rich get all the breaks and the poor catch all the hell. What can be greater than you calling all the shots? You may have to wear many different hats in the beginning and make much sacrifice, but your end results will speak for themselves. Everything that I have ever accomplished and been congratulated for has come from hard work and dedication. Being devoted to my ideas and having the will to act upon them is how my ideas manifest.

Exercise your faith by being who you were created to be. Everybody has a gift and many purposes. This is the stage where you boss up. Whatever has been on your agenda, put one foot in front of the other and rise to the occasion. Anybody can work a nine-to-five job and support themselves, but what are your contributions to society? What makes you great? Give life your all. In everything you do, make it great. Normal people do normal things. Extraordinary people stand out by being the best versions of themselves. There's no honor in being ordinary. Be your greatest so you will inspire those who already know that they are destined for greatness. Your purpose in life is big, and your potential has always been great.

The world is waiting for you. In the exciting world of entrepreneurship, you call all the shots. There is nothing more liberating than being on vacation and not having to worry about where your next dollar is coming from. You'll have more freedom and independence working for yourself. Once your business is firmly established, you will have the flexibility to make sure you don't miss the events and moments that matter the most in your life.

> There is no passion to be found playing small—in settling for a life that is less than the one you are capable of living.
>
> —Nelson Mandela

It's not time to be tired. It's time to rise up and face all your fears and doubts. Your journey in life has already provided you with strength, courage, and knowledge. Don't be deceived by your own mind. There is something in everyone's brain that says, "It's too hard" or "It can't be accomplished," every time we want to accomplish something great. There are two types of people in the world, the type who will listen to the negativity and doubts and the type who, in spite of doubt, will still reach a hand out and try to accomplish it. Be the person who reaches a hand out.

Be a person of action because it's bigger than you. People are watching you. Be the best for your children, nieces, and nephews. When your mind is focused and made up, don't make excuses. If you fail, try again. Bring your ideas to life, even if you must push beyond the limits. A journey of a thousand miles begins with one step. If you want something to work badly enough, you will find a way to make it work.

Have a champion mindset. Be ready to defeat or surpass all rivals. Don't underestimate yourself; that will lead to procrastination. Exercise determination and a will to succeed. All businessmen must have courage and a fighting spirit. Every defeat, every heartbreak, and every loss contains its own seed, its own lesson on how to improve your performance the next time. So be bold, bad, and wiser. Focus on your goals, not your obstacles. You need to be mentally prepared to deal with the challenges and sacrifices that comes along with business ownership.

Entrepreneurs have the opportunity to shape the future with new ideas, inspiration, and positive motivation. There is no excuse. If the next man can do it, then so can you. You are the reason that you live a life of mediocrity. Nobody can stop you from accomplishing anything— nobody but the man in the mirror. Critique your ambitions and move forward with confidence. Do it for your ambitions. Do it for your inner man, who is the greatest part of you. The flesh may get weary and the mind might get tired sometimes, but there's always a hero inside of you. I know you feel it just like I do. It's something about you. Your name belongs in lights. The world is supposed to know your name. Make your mark in this life and embrace all challenges. Wisdom will come from the experiences. The challenges are what makes life interesting, and overcoming them is what makes life meaningful.

You can't secure a bag with jet lag. Be self-motivated. Don't nobody care if you become a boss until you become a boss. You will get all the respect you deserve, just like anybody else who is being the best version of themselves.

Stay physically and mentally fit. Get plenty of exercise, discipline your diet, and learn new skills—they exercise the brain. Most successful people strive for perfection in all areas of their lives, not just at the office.

Be sharp. In order to rise to the occasion, you have to look the part, know the part, and act the part. You have the leading role, so make it a box-office hit.

Be confident. When you believe in yourself, you don't have to convince others. If you build it, they will come. By the time they realize your worth, you'll be worth more.

The so-called Blackman is not lacking in education; he's lacking the will to build for himself. Use your degree to create your own stream of revenue, instead of making someone else richer. If you can create one or two jobs in your own community, it's worth it.

Stop thinking and acting like an inferior person. We must come out of the spirit of depending on others to do for us what we must do for ourselves. You can't say that you are a free man and don't want the responsibility of freedom. We must rise up and take our lives into our own hands. We must stop waiting for crumbs to fall off of someone else's table. You are the only people who have never received reparations or anything to get started on. It's obvious that they don't love you. They expect you to pull yourself up by your own bootstraps.

Although some of us were here first, we're strangers in a land that is not our own. This country was built on the backs of our ancestors. We still suffer today from the systematic oppression that began postslavery. There is no deportation for a so-called African American; you go straight to prison, a slave ship on land.

Blacks have a tremendous spending power. Today our spending power exceeds $ 1 trillion. Collectively as Black Americans, we're richer than most countries. Our only solution is to come together in some common cause and stop wasting our resources. We must build for ourselves. If we are organized, we can change our own destiny. We have to get to the position where we can take pride in what we produce.

By spending our money among one another, we will build our own economic power base. We need to buy land. Once our money circulates in our own community a few times, we will be able to build a future for our children—our own schools, hospitals, and grocery stores. People come from faraway countries just to study us and our spending habits. Ever notice how Arab Americans will sell fried chicken in your neighborhoods although they don't eat fried chicken?

There's a saying that money in a Black person's hand is like liquid gold. You spend it just as fast as you make it. So they study you from afar, come to America, and pitch their tent. They set up shop. And although you've been in this country longer than many of them, they surpass you economically. We must prepare our children for economic self-development. College doesn't guarantee you a job or an opportunity. The top 1 percent never went to college.

We're at the bottom, but we spend more than those on top. We have to stop being selfish and thinking only of ourselves. We have to start passing down wealth to the next generation. They will have nothing to get started with unless you have a business or wealth to leave them.

College creates debt, and our children are already starting out behind the eight ball. Black people must start doing for themselves. In order for us to catch up, we must run faster.

Stop thinking that America needs you to work its jobs in order to be successful. They will send you to prison. Stop acting like police brutality doesn't exist. When you face the facts and deal with reality, you will know how to get in line and come up with a strategy to get out of the situation that we're in.

I value education, so if you can afford to put your child through college, by all means do so. We need people in every position. My people are destroyed by lack of knowledge. Make sure you tell your children you didn't send them to college to leave their community. Tell them to use their knowledge for the betterment of their community. We must make a collective vocation to build and develop our community in order to restore our people to their traditional greatness.

There's a Black family-owned construction firm headquartered in Philadelphia, Pennsylvania. Mr. Darrell K. Coats Sr, his father, his son, and his grandson are doing big things. Most importantly, they're all in business together. That's four generations of wealth. They manage large-scale development projects, construct senior living residences, and provide technologically advanced SaaS platforms to create smart cities. They plan to create jobs in the cities they service.

Mr. Coats had a vision, came up with a plan, and executed it well. He was named Minority Contractor of the Year in 2011 and has won other awards as well. He's also involved with nonprofit organizations that run biweekly food drives. He has a hand in several endeavors, and he's an all-around genuinely good person. He has made many contributions, and his goal is to continue to support organizations and social causes that move us forward. He's a good example of a generational wealth builder and visionary.

Also, new Black Wall Street marketplaces have opened in Georgia. One is in Stonecrest. I love the concept of a new Black Wall Street. Our history is empowering. It brings to light everything that we're capable of accomplishing. These stories must be given to our children and their children, because as long as you can be convinced that you never did anything, you can never do anything.

We're not a genetically inferior race of people. We're gifted, we're talented, and we're incredible achievers. We are the fathers of many inventions. During slavery it was illegal for a Black person to own a patent, so we never received credit for many of our ideas and inventions. Our contributions to society are tremendous. We owe the world nothing.

CHAPTER 3

MAKE IT HAPPEN

DON'T BURY YOUR TALENT. NOBODY respects you when you're nonproductive. Surely you weren't created to work for somebody else your entire life. That's their legacy, not yours. There are only 186 hours in a week. You spend the majority of your time working and commuting back and forth to work. You spend the other time with your partner or children. You seldom have time for a vacation. What about you and who you were created to be? What about your purpose? What happened to your aspirations, your dreams, your visions? Where there are no visions, people perish. What happened to that book you wanted to write? What are you doing with your art? What's stopping you from opening a restaurant? Believe it or not your destined to do greater things in life then you have already accomplished.

There's a biblical story of three servants and their master. Before going on a long trip, he gave each servant some money according to their abilities. One invested the master's money and made double. Another servant put the money in the bank, and it grew in interest. Out of fear that he would blow the money, the third servant buried the money. The master was well pleased with the two servants who used their minds to increase the amount of money he gave them. They were productive. The third servant was cast away because he did nothing to grow his money.

You are just one decision away from a totally different life. It's your time to become the head and not the tail. Don't ever think it's too late to turn your life around. It's never too late. Quit talking and start doing. A self-made person depends on his or her own hands to create, not on someone else to provide. Your energy is currency, so spend it wisely. You're not living your best life until you first accomplish something. Every day is not a celebration or a party. Most people who turn up all the time are oppressed. It takes a focused mind and determination to be successful. So, when successful people raise their glasses for a toast, it's well deserved, and they are not living a delusion.

CHAPTER 4

POSSIBILITIES

DON'T TRY TO FIT INTO someone else's box. Always be productive, and invest continually in your business. People will not understand why you do the things you do. Business is not for everyone, so they won't comprehend. Move in silence because you don't need the negativity around you or something or someone trying to tire you in the process. Stick to what you know, and don't believe everything others tell you. People don't always like to see others succeed, so don't announce your next move. Just do it.

Before I founded Emerald Enterprise Corporation, I worked for Apple as a technical support representative. It was a great company to work for, but I had my own ideas, and Apple was consuming all my time. I had laid the blueprint for my own business before I was employed by Apple, but like most people, I was used to receiving a sure check. I was comfortable bringing in money and paying bills, but I wasn't happy with myself. I had begun to feel like a slave because I wasn't accomplishing anything but helping someone else get rich. I was tired of someone else's cause. So, I had to face my fears and not settle, all the what-ifs and all the reasons I won't just quit this job. I was so used to being in the workforce, but with contracts signed, I had to take that leap of faith. I didn't understand most things about running a business, so it took more than faith. It takes knowledge and applying oneself to the task at hand.

I didn't have a lot of money saved for this endeavor, but it was now or never. I told my wife that I was about to quit my job and start my own business. I did not know exactly what she might say, but I was pretty confident that she would support me 100 percent. I worked three more days, and finally the chains were loosened. The day that I finally quit my job, I immediately went to work for myself. Even though I still had obstacles to face, I knew that I couldn't sit still. I don't believe in sitting still. Besides, I still had bills to be paid. I let all the what-ifs go and took a step forward. I created a website and began hiring employees to service Fortune 500 jobs. I created an employment agency. Within thirty days of quitting my job, I had thirty employees.

Although every business operates differently, you must have support and be willing to sacrifice. I was willing to do whatever it took to get my business up and running. But my will alone was not enough. I needed people around me who understood things about business that I did not. When you get sick and tired of being sick and tired, you will push forward and create your own opportunity instead of waiting for one to be presented. I didn't visualize myself being a boss, but I have always felt good about myself. I have always known that it's something special about me. I've always known that I was put on this earth to do great things in life. How you think of yourself will be your outcome. The energy that you put out into the world is the same energy you will receive.

Remember: In every great work there will be obstacles, and if it comes too easily, it probably won't work. All things are possible if you are willing to work hard and stay focused. Nothing is impossible if your willing learn and work hard. Think big!

> Impossible is just a big word thrown around by small men who find it easier to live in the world they have been given than to explore the power they have to change it.
>
> Impossible is not a fact. It's an opinion. Impossible is not a declaration. It's a dare. Impossible is potential. Impossible is temporary.
>
> —Muhammad Ali

Don't waste your time or energy worrying about who doesn't support you. They are not worth the conversation. As I mentioned earlier, not everyone will support you, so be good to your customers and employees, and they will be good to you. Be loyal over a little first, and the increase will find you. You will eventually become the ruler of much. You don't need everybody's support. Find ways to make the customers you already become loyal. Promote your brand until it's implanted in your audience's subconscious. If you use social media to advertise, make sure every time, they login they see your logo. When I first started out in business, people tested my integrity. They would ask, "This isn't a scam, is it?" At first, I got upset and would think, *Scam? This me, and I have never been a shady individual. They must not know me.* In all actuality, they didn't know who I was because I was dealing on a whole other level. I didn't need to prove myself to people who knew me already because I was prejudged by them. All I needed were people who needed my service.

People want something and someone they can trust and believe in. But in today's times, there are so many scammers it's hard to accept what's really real when it's right in front of you. You must always be professional, even if people get under your skin. "A warrior fights with courage and not with anger." It's always about business, so act accordingly. Just because people don't know who you are doesn't mean that you are not somebody. Your ideas alone have gotten you this far. "People with small minds talk about people, people with average minds talk about events, and people with above average minds talk about ideas."

Along my business journey I spoke with a gentleman who's part of a very successful marketing business. I told him of my ideas and how I was the architect of two businesses. Once I laid my blueprints out before him, he replied, "Well you don't need us for much at all. Just the marketing. I would rather talk to you than talk to millionaires because some of the millionaires I talk to only have money but no business ideas or how to invest their money." In this world you have two types of people: the ones who just talk, and the ones who are doers. If you want something bad enough you will go after it. Speak less and do more. Don't be a talker; be a doer. Separate yourself from those who don't want something out of life. Don't allow yourself to be consumed with things that are not in your best interest of rising to the top.

If you want to be a businessperson then politic with other people who are about business. Building a foundation takes time, so if you don't have patience, then business is not for you. A well-drawn business plan is wonderful, but you must be willing to do what it takes to execute that plan. Everything will not always go as planned, but if you are persistent about what you believe in, then one day it will unfold. Every day won't be sunny, but it's not going to rain every day either. Don't be someone who the world thought you couldn't be. Be the person that you know you are. Think without falling asleep. Mind your business! If it's important to you, you will make the time. If it's not important to you, you will make excuses. Don't focus on more than one thing at a time. Focus on what you are more passionate about. The mind is capable of coming up with all sorts of brilliant ideas, but all business plans take time and money to execute. Stay focused on the tasks at hand. It's not going to happen overnight. You must be devoted to developing a foundation for your business. Self-belief and hard work will earn you success. Whatever the mind can conceive and believe can be achieved. The people you hire to help you with your business must believe in you and at some point, be able to see your vision. You can't do it all by yourself. You will need a marketing department, human resources, payroll, and so much more. It depends on what type of business you own, but you will definitely need help. The journey begins at the finish line. Right now, you're building.

CHAPTER 5

THE FUTURE IS NOW

YOU ARE THE FUTURE, NOT the children, because they're only going to do what they see you do—no more and no less. You create your own DNA by what you practice. If your children never see you accomplish anything great, it's likely they will live lives of mediocrity. Change starts at home, and it starts with you. Save the adults and you save the future. Save the man-child.

The battlefield is in the mind. Do what is best to preserve the mind. Continuously searching for pleasure is a waste of a grown man's life. A drunk mind will never be all that it was created to be. There's nothing wrong with celebrating your accomplishments, but getting drunk all the time and calling it a vibe is a lie. It's a problem.

Working can be stressful, and working for someone else doesn't make it any better. It's labor. Your job has priority over your family and everything that you love. If a man doesn't work, he doesn't eat. But you don't have to work for someone else your entire life. How about someone working for you? You can do whatever you want to do if you apply yourself. Never stop believing, no matter what anybody says. Be the best at what you do, and live your best life. If the next man can do it, so can you.

My son Jamal is a full-time photographer. He didn't start out that way. Of course in the beginning he had a different full-time job and did photography on the side. Now he's proud to say that his business pays the bills and he manages his own time. Every move he makes is on his own terms. He's able to take more vacations. He is free. The chances of his son becoming a businessowner is great. If not, whatever he does will be great.

You are the future, and the future is now. Your life is an expression. At some point you will inspire others, whether positively or negatively. When you give it your all and walk in your purpose, your children will feel compelled to do the same thing. You're actually transferring energy.

Tomorrow isn't promised to anybody. The future is an illusion. It's not for certain. You have freedom of choice—not tomorrow, but today. Whatever you put your hand to, do your best, because people are watching. Your children are watching. "Do not follow where the path may lead, go instead where there is no path and leave a trail."

Your attitude and actions must reflect the philosophy "Succeed or die trying." If you are reading this, nine times out of ten you are chosen. You know that your life was meant for more than just working from nine to five. Who are you inspiring? Make a difference by leaving a different path. How do you expect the next generation to believe in themselves if you don't give them a good example? It's all about information. You must do things differently if you expect a different result. Teach differently, and maybe your children will listen to what you have to say. We have to be willing to create our own jobs instead of depending on society to do it for us.

The next generation is affected by the decisions that you make. Instead of going to college, getting a degree, and then helping make somebody else richer, use your education to build, educate, and give back to your own community. Go the extra mile. Your light shows the path for those around you. Teach them about Black Wall Street. Now is not the time to be quiet. Teach them about the Moors. Teach them about all of those who were conquerors before us. Teach them that those conquerors were us. Teach them all that is empowering. We have a rich culture and history beyond the slave ships. Don't let slavery and oppression be the only story they know. When you know who you are, nobody has to like you or respect you. A king isn't bothered by what a peasant thinks of him.

If you are concerned about the future, look in the mirror, because you're it. The time is now. Be all that you can. Do all that you can and the children will do the same. Let people do whatever they need to do to be happy. Mind your business and do what you need to do. Be the change that you would like to see. Your life is important, and you're a role model to more people than you know.

Knowing your worth is your superpower. Take good care of yourself physically, mentally, and spiritually. You are the future, and the world needs more people like you. Nothing about you is average. You're already great, but you must know it and believe it to act like it.

Don't trap yourself with the idea of a future. You would accomplish more if the word *future* had never been invented. When you do become obsessed by the future, you create distance between you and that which you think you need or should have. If you want something, call it into existence and it will be. If you speak positively, your actions will be in a positive direction. If you deal with negativity, it will drain you, and your actions will become hopeless. If you want someone to be proud of you, all you have to do is be proud—not in arrogance, but in your thoughts and your actions.

Don't let the nine to five consume you to the point that there is nothing left of you. You will die tired and unfulfilled. Being accomplished and successful according to the standards of the Western world is not all that there is. Your life will have no impact on the next generation if you choose to do absolutely nothing. Anybody can get a job and make a living. What's on the inside of you wants to break free. Break the hex off.

If you think you were created to work for someone else your entire life, this book probably isn't for you. That's not freedom. There's nothing liberating about it. You're helping to make someone else rich. That person will replace you in a heartbeat if they feel like it.

You are your own security for your present life. It doesn't matter what kind of business you consider doing. Whatever it is, it will leave an impression and impact on the next generation. We have to start somewhere. Do it for your sons and daughters. Each one teach one. Do it for your nieces and nephews and everyone who is blessed to be in your presence. Your potentials are great. There is nothing you cannot accomplish. You are your ancestors with the power of gods.

Make power moves and don't sleep on your own potential. That's what they want you to do, so you will be docile and complaisant. You weren't put here on earth to work on the assembly line. You have a purpose, and it is great. But it's up to you to know what that is.

What are you passionate about and do kinda well? Start there! You weren't created for nothing. You have a purpose. The energy that you put out will be transferred to those closest to you first. If you smoke and drink your life away, your kids will come up the same way. If they see positive moves that you're making, they will make positive moves themselves. Every moment that we spend in higher consciousness helps uplift the consciousness of the whole world.

You have the power to change the world. The more you channel your energy in the right direction, the quicker the things you're trying to accomplish will manifest. The longer you procrastinate, the more time it will take to manifest. You were born to be creative and use your own mind. Teach your children early in life about limited liability corporations and ownership. A child will learn at whatever level you teach them.

You don't need a high school diploma to start your own business. You need an idea. Expand your mind. Step into the now and make moves. What you do today is your tomorrow. You are responsible not only for your life, but those who are watching you as well.

It's all energy. Look at me as your subconscious speaking to you. This energy is supreme. You are the beginning and the end. If you can't join them, then beat them. You gotta get up and be somebody. You can either stay inside your head or let your light shine. Keep planting seeds. The subconscious minds of others are awake, even if their conscious minds are asleep. Not everyone will get it, but the right ones will hear you differently.

We are vibrational beings of light and energy. Our energy cannot be destroyed; it can only be transformed from one form to another. I watched my dad run his own business, and for a long time I didn't have any desire to run my own business. Positive energy is contagious.

Give others hope through your actions. It's up to you to bring about hope and change in your community. Be that positive influence that they're waiting to see. Teaching our children about Abraham Lincoln or George Washington isn't empowering. According to surviving documentation, at least twelve presidents were slave owners at some point during their lives. Teach your children about Nat Turner, Marcus Garvey, Malcolm X, Stokely Carmichael, Huey P. Newton, and Harriet Tubman. Teach them about all our freedom fighters. Teach them about all the Black inventors. Teach them about the civilization the Moors brought to Spain from North Africa. Teach them about all the empowering things. Embrace your strengths and your intelligence. You're a warrior; it's in your DNA.

A dream is your creative vision for your life in what you call the future. To achieve a dream, you must break out of your current comfort zone and become comfortable with the unfamiliar. Step out on faith. Remove the mountain that hinders your present life from being productive. Be who you want to be. It's wise to plan, but sometimes you have to just do it. Don't be so critical. Stop overthinking. One thing will lead to another. It's all positive.

You don't have time to be cautious. Don't look for reasons not to move forward. After so long, it's cowardly. God has not given us the spirit of fear but of love, courage, and a sound mind. Learn not to be frightened or distressed about your so-called future. Today is important. Deal with the now. Be productive today and tomorrow will handle itself. Don't settle for what life has given you; make your life better by building. You create your own reality.

Some people keep trying to look into the future, while history keeps repeating itself. Fashion repeats itself. Music repeats itself. You celebrate the same traditional holidays at the same time of year every year until you die.

Which pill are you going to take? It's not you against the world; it's you versus yourself.

You'll settle for a job if you don't have a dream.

—Damien J. Moss Sr

The moment you change your perception is the moment your world changes. It all starts in the mind. People with small minds talk about people. People with average minds talk about events. People with above-average minds talk about ideas. Who you are today is who you are going to be tomorrow. You can either worry about the future or make better choices today. Your outcome will be in direct proportion to your contribution.

Sometimes other people can see your potential before you can because they're not weighing up the cost. Don't set yourself up for failure by worrying if something won't work out.

Be who you were born to be. Anything that I've accomplished or have does not make me somebody. As a child I knew that I was somebody. I would rather get paid less for doing something that I love and am passionate about than have a title. It's called purpose. Find out what you like to do and are kinda good at. The most important two days of your life are the day you were born and the day you found out why. It's in the why where you find peace and true happiness. That thing makes you feel complete and accomplished. You take pride in it. It is your light that helps others see there's hope.

What you do causes others to believe in themselves. Bless the world with creativity. Inspire others by being the best version of yourself. You cannot take pleasure in doing nothing. You were born to live and not die. Be prosperous and in good health even as your soul prospers. Where is your time and energy going? The mind is a terrible thing to waste. The mind controls the body. If you don't program your own mind, it will be programmed for you. The minds of the masses are consumed with stuff they don't need, unhealthy and entertaining. It's a circus trying to keep up with the Joneses.

If you have to spend money on material things you don't need to get the validation of others, you need a hug. Self-esteem is the number-one characteristic you must have in order to be successful at anything. Self-esteem is crucial to your true happiness—well, let me say joy, because joy is everlasting. Would you be proud to say that you work for a Fortune 500 company? When you die, do you think the president of the company will attend your funeral and show his respect for all the years of service that you gave him? Or shut down the company for a day in your remembrance?

Everybody has to eat. Yes, I understand that. But that's not your purpose in life. You're better than that. Don't physically leave this earth with your purpose unfulfilled. (I say *physical* because your energy will remain.) The people are watching. It's never too late to start your own business, get a degree or write a book and become a best-selling author. But you have to start somewhere. Stay in your lane even if it seems like others are passing you.

> Be patient and stay focused. Don't let comparisons become a distraction. You will arrive to your destination. Unlock your potential and achieve your goals.
>
> —Keela Swinson

More and more people are quitting their jobs every day to pursue their passions. If you build it, they will come. Don't allow others to control the direction of your life. Find your own path. Think positive and make sure your actions align with your thoughts. The world needs who you were truly created to be. You control your own destiny. There is so much more to you than what kind of car you drive or the clothes you wear. The world is looking for somebody who is genuine and driven. Your energy will spark the lives around you. You are an inspiration and a force of motivation. Stop spending money on things you don't need to impress people who really don't care. You will become bitter if you continuously compete with others. Compete with yourself so that you will become better.

Open your mind to the world of knowledge and information. It takes less than death to kill a man. What happened to your dreams and aspirations? Take a shot at life and all that the universe may want to offer you. Life is short, so spend it on something worthy and worthwhile. Be great. Don't condemn yourself for your mistakes. Stay focused and stick to whatever it is you would like to accomplish. It's a jungle we're living in, and nobody is exempt from temptation and temporary care.

Do what you're supposed to do when you're supposed to do it. Work hard and stay committed. It shall come to pass. Stop worrying about who you want to become and look at the person you already are. If you stay focused, you will continuously make progress.

When you love doing something, you will make time for it. If not, you will make excuses. Challenge your fears and attempt to accomplish what your heart desires. You have one life to live, so shine and be great.

Your wealth is wrapped up inside of your purpose. There is nothing more rewarding than finding your purpose and walking in it. No material thing or money can satisfy your soul like accomplishing what you have set out to do. You can move mountains if only you believe. Be passionate because the time is now—not tomorrow, next week or maybe down the road. If you waste your life away, your kids will come up the same way. It's bigger than you. Now is the time.

You hold the keys to your own desires. How bad do you want it? If you don't start today, then when? Everything you do today determines your future, so your future is now. Don't hesitate and don't procrastinate. You are a leader. You were born to win. You're not the tail; you are the head.

When a person thinks big, they accomplish big things. It all starts in the mind with your belief system. It's easy to succeed when you have a strong belief system. Anything a person truly believes in will make a way. Take back your energy and your existence. Be who you wanna be and not who society has programmed you to be.

Strive to do big things, so those who are watching will believe in themselves. You have the power to change lives just the way you are. We need more entrepreneurs and good role models. If we don't show people, how are they supposed to know? If you don't show the next generation a better way, it will deteriorate. Your responsibility is to be the best you can be. They're watching you, hoping for a king. You have the power.

> For I know the plans I have for you; plans to prosper
> you and not to harm you, plans to give you a hope and
> a future.

> —Jeremiah 29:11

You are under divine pressure because you're birthing something great. It's not always going to feel good while you're in the process. Run and don't get weary. Walk but do not faint. Your joy will overflow continuously. Keep the faith. Know your worth. Don't be afraid to shine. Who lights a candle and hides it under a basket? Take a chance on yourself and be that light.

Don't downplay yourself because you don't fit in. Have the courage to be disliked. Don't apologize for being yourself. The world needs more authenticity. Don't bury your talents. You are gifted and equipped with everything you need for your journey. It's already in you—strength, courage, and knowledge.

Don't let anything stop you from reaching your goal. Fear is an illusion. Stop worrying about stuff that may or may not happen. Move forward and you will begin to create your own opportunities. Nothing from nothing leaves nothing, but positive energy activates constant elevation.

Mind the business that pays you. Mind the business that is in your best interest and enhances your direction and purpose. Your purpose is important. Purpose is that void that a lot of people can't fill. They search for it in relationships, material things, and plenty of self-indulgence, but they are never content. They're not free. They live from day to day on a hamster wheel, constantly moving and not going anywhere. Many have lived and died with their purpose unfulfilled. No action is too small. The richest soil is in the cemetery, where dreams, lives, and ideas are buried.

If running your own business won't bring you fulfillment, then by all means find your creative sense and bring to life that which is your essence. Bring to life the vision in your mind. Let nothing destroy the beauty of your dream. Believe in yourself and your ideas. It's up to you and nobody else to make your dreams a reality. Don't stress or overthink it. You got it! Work toward your purpose. Walk in your purpose. Believe in your purpose.

Don't worry about anything. Deal with situations when they come up. Effort is a direct reflection of interest. If you want to accomplish more in life than the average person, you will know your worth and act accordingly. Know what you deserve in life and act accordingly. Don't settle for less. Trust the process. The strongest factor in success is your self-confidence—believing you can do it, believing you deserve it, and believing that you will accomplish it. Keep thinking and stay involved. One thing will lead to another. Don't let fear manifest itself as procrastination. Kill it!

Deal with the present only. Tomorrow has problems of its own. If you make one wheel turn, the other wheels will turn right along with it. So let up on the brakes and be great. Know that you are capable of anything. Don't spend your entire life being a big thinker but living in survival mode.

The world needs to see a positive force like you. In order for the minds around you to change, they must first see a change. So be that change that you're hoping to see. We're in desperate need of a change. While you're procrastinating, the people around you are hurting. There is no hope if they can't see it. Hope deferred makes the heart sick, but when there is hope, there is life. There is life inside of your purpose. Purpose isn't for self-gratification, but for you to use to inspire others.

Purpose involves work and alone time. Purpose is not in your past. Purpose is you right now in your present condition. What are you afraid of? Bust a move. Do something. Whatever you do, don't do nothing.

Purpose is not posting pictures on Facebook. Purpose is your greatest praise. Purpose is your essence and deepest inner being. Put your name on it. Speak things as if they are, even when they are not. Call forth your best life. Speak positively about yourself. Fear and doubt are illusions.

Don't waste time with family and friends who are not purpose driven. The only person you ought to be FaceTiming is yourself. You're wasting precious time and energy. Be creative. You were born to show the world something. Run, Forrest, run! If you feel some type of way, get over it. Your life is wasting away. The safety is off. Pull the trigger—you might as well!

You're alive, but you're not truly living until you stand up and be who God created you to be. A comfort zone is a beautiful place, but nothing ever grows there. No matter what you may be going through in your life, you have a purpose. Don't be afraid to give up the good to go for the great. You feel unsettled because you know you are meant for more. Stop settling!

Be your own biggest fan, your own biggest believer, and put it on your back and carry the weight.

—Nipsey Hussle

You don't have to be perfect to walk in your purpose. You don't have to be a business owner, musician, preacher, or singer. Each person has their own unique personality, talents, and gifts. Laziness is the Blackman's worst sin.

The day you were born don't mean anything unless you make it mean something. If you do nothing, you will be nothing. The only thing that makes the day you were born special is what you do with your life. People will mark the day that you were born as significant because you had an impact on human beings. Hold your head up and know that you're somebody. You're beautiful, brothers and sisters. You're intelligent and wise. There is no reason you shouldn't have all that your heart desires.

You will be surprised who's watching your journey and being inspired by it. Don't settle when it comes to your life. If you don't go after what you want, you will never have it. If you do not ask, the answer will always be no. If you do not step forward, you will remain in the same place.

> I believe there is a time and situation in every person's life for them to be great. In that moment of greatness our purpose on earth is revealed. Some people let their moment slip by and they are stuck here unable to discern their purpose. I feel a tug at times as though I have unfinished business and at other times I feel spent and drained. Sick of this skin I'm in but too much of a

coward to peek through the veil. There is a voice inside me tho … keeps saying my best is yet to come!

—Talib Abu Saad

People who don't have the same vision you do will never understand why you work so hard or distance yourself at times. It's called purpose. You can't afford to be doing just anything with anybody. Your time and your name are on the line.

Your role as a leader is to bring out the best in others without even trying to. Pay attention to what's happening in your life and don't try to interrupt the process. Anybody can decide to do nothing with their life, but not you. Reach like you've never reached before so you can touch what you never touched before. Let your world see something it's never seen before. Don't let anything stop you from shining.

The million-dollar question we ask children is "What do you wanna be when you grow up?" You are the only one who can limit your greatness. You are the source. You can either get involved or let life pass you by. Are you a player or a spectator?

The gap between the life you want and the life you are living is called mindset, focus, and consistency. You were meant to be more than mediocre. It's time to blow some minds and break belief systems. Let go of your fear and go after everything you want. Become fearless and your life becomes limitless. Think about what makes you happy and be productive with it.

In order for you to be great, you must be concerned with the lives of others. How you live your life will call others to action. The mission of the entrepreneur is not only to make his pockets fat but to inspire others to rise up and do the same. Why is generational wealth important? Wealth gives you more options in life. You have more freedom to think and live the life you want when you don't have to worry about paying your bills. There are different ways of building generational wealth: real estate, creating a business, the stock market, and education.

CHAPTER 6

MENTAL HEALTH IS WEALTH

THE MIND IS A TERRIBLE thing to waste. You can choose to do nothing with your life, but it will be costly. Have dignity. Take hold of yourself and focus on what's important in life. Your health is wealth. Successful people are well-rounded. They understand that to create a successful life, they must live long enough to enjoy the fruits of their labor.

Everybody isn't on your level. Don't waste time and energy in conversations with people who are not visionaries like you. Keep your business to yourself. Some people are like vampires. They're trying to suck the life out of you. They never have anything good to say. You can't afford to be mentally engaged with something that's pulling in the opposite direction from where you're trying to go. Know the difference between constructive criticism versus someone who never has anything good to say. Protect your energy. People will try to dim your light. We're not all headed in the same direction. You have to do what's best for you. Understand the assignment and move in confidence. This is something you have to do for yourself. Being an entrepreneur is all about rocking the boat.

You have to go against the grain and take risks. It's your vision, and for that reason alone, people will never understand your moves. It's not always going to be easy. You will face ups and downs. If you ever feel uncomfortable or have doubts, understand that you are breaking molds. Starting a business is a hard step to take. Have faith in your convictions and the service or products that you are introducing to the world. "Be mindful of your self-talk, its your conversation with the universe." What you create in your mind, you can create in your reality. Speak life and not death upon your situation. Speak prosperity and not poverty. Life and death are in the power of the tongue.

There's nothing you cannot accomplish. It's just a matter of applying yourself. Don't ignore your own potential. Eliminate what doesn't help you evolve—including people. If someone wants to see you become successful, they will help you become successful. It's optimally up to you to conceive and internalize what you're trying to accomplish.

The eyes are useless when the mind is blind. Mental health is important, so distance yourself from all negativity and drama. Beautiful things will begin to happen in your life. One who believes in oneself has no need to convince others. Yes, you will face challenges, but being defeated is optional. You never have to give up—that's a choice. These are your dreams, so don't let anybody talk you out of what's important to you. Your happiness is worth pursuing. You only have one life to live, so make it count.

You have the power to inspire others, so live your life to the fullest. Don't settle for a job your entire life. The way the internet is set up, you can network without leaving your home. There are currently 9.1 million online retailers in the world, and 2.5 million of them are in the United

E. KINNARD MOSS

States. If you have something that you think you're good at, now is the perfect time to market your brand. If you want something to happen, you have to make it happen. Don't overthink things. Just do it.

Get outside of your own head; sometimes that's the worse place to be. Sometimes the best thing you can do is not think, not wonder. Don't obsess or even imagine. Just take a deep breath and have faith that everything will work out for the best.

You know that you're different from others. If you're cut from a different piece of cloth, make it all line up. Make power moves and play your part. Don't waste precious time with people who don't have goals. There is nothing to gain from it. But be humble enough to know that you're not better than anyone else.

Your life is precious. It's a vapor—here one moment and gone the next. Don't put effort into those who show no effort toward you. There's only so much you can do before you're wasting your time and energy. If you want something out of life, you don't have time for people. Ordinary people do ordinary things their entire lives. They may speak of brilliant ideas, but they will never make a real effort to accomplish anything. Anyone can choose to do nothing with their life. Don't be so selfish.

Strive to reach your full potential in life and your children will do the same. You are their first inspiration. If you're not a positive influence for them, what type of outcome do you expect? If you bury your talents, they will bury theirs. You can't expect more out of them. That's costly!

> A coward and a hero feel the same. Its what they do that
> makes them different. The hero feels just as frightened
> as the coward. Its what he does that makes him a hero,

and what the other fellow doesn't do that makes him a coward.

—Cus D'Amato

Sometimes you will feel isolated and alone. This is much needed, so you can gather your thoughts and see clearly. Sometimes your circle decreases in size but increases in value. You gotta do this for you. This isn't about anybody else. You won't have any regrets if you give 110 percent to everything you put your hand to. Possibilities are limitless when you have a dog in the fight. No matter how you feel, you must not let fear hold you back. It may require new levels of courage, confidence and consistency, so stay determined.

Success is not built on success. Everything will not always work out. There are mistakes to be made, and practice leads to perfection. Think positively and things will work for you. It's really that simple. If you want something to work for you badly enough, it will happen—no matter what it is. So don't worry. Once you take the first step, you will know what it is you need to do next.

Life is too short to wake up with regrets, so believe in everything that you do. Set goals. Doing so will help guide your focus. Setting goals is good for your overall mental health. When you set goals, it gives you momentum for life. Don't find yourself in the same place doing the exact same thing next year.

We're living in a world full of superficial thrills. Nothing is really what it appears to be. Everybody is a boss on the surface and living their best life. Don't be fooled by illusions. People's lives are empty, and they don't know what it is they're missing. Social media gives people a false since of pride and an exit from reality. Most have forsaken their purpose in life for selfies and interactions with people who don't have a life. People are not living; they only exist. Life is meaningless when you're void of purpose. You have nothing that you're working toward or trying to accomplish. You only exist.

You work hard and spend your hard-earned money on commercial items to make you feel good about yourself and the life that you're living. When a person loves themselves, they give 100 percent to their entire creation. You were born to create and be productive. You were born to be driven and passionate. But somewhere in time, you let your fuel run out. Now is the time for you to knock the dust off your heels, pick yourself up, and find your creative force.

You have the ability to change lives. The energy you give to positively change your life is the same energy that will cause others to live a purpose-filled life. Energy doesn't die; it's only transferred.

Don't let life fool you into thinking that your dreams and ambitions are not important. You're important! Your business is important. Your art is important. Your music is important. Doing the right thing is never wrong. Even if you're not successful, it's better to try than not to try at all. You will inspire the youthful minds.

The hardest thing to do is to get started. I have been approached numerous times for advice about writing a book. People have many questions, and they always say that they want to write about their lives. Many people know exactly what they want to do. It's the unknown that keeps them from moving forward. One thing leads to another, but you have to put it into motion. Life's exciting and full of opportunities, so make your presence known. If you start today, you can accomplish whatever you put your mind to and have a good life.

Don't worry about the past or future. You have no control over that. Some people live in the past with regrets of doing nothing with their lives. Don't be that person. Life is full of beauty, magic, and surprises. Level up and manifest your higher self. Love yourself and live life with passion and purpose. Be the best version of yourself you know how to be.

> There is no greater gift you can give or receive than to honor your calling. Its why you were born. And how you become most truly alive.
>
> —Oprah Winfrey

Let nothing and nobody hinder your progress. Value your time and energy. Today will never come again, so stay self-motivated and in motion. You have a higher purpose, so recognize who you are and strive to be great. Do not be self-indulgent. Get rid of all things that keep you from being effective in your calling or profession. Do what's necessary to maintain high self-esteem. Diet and exercise. When you look good, you feel good. You need to have a healthy mind and body and an appetite to succeed.

Expect greatness from yourself and the world will compliment you. Don't get caught up in things; that's not good for your mental health. This world has a way of making you feel like giving up or think that you're the only one who's purpose driven. That's a lie. Your purpose was the reason you were born. You're not missing anything that's going on in this world.

Stay driven and devoted to your ideas. Mind your own business and walk in your calling. Stay focused because nobody knows what you need to do but you. Don't lay down your life and just be that ordinary person. Reach for the stars, touch the sky, and kiss the moon. The time is now, and it's your time.

People are not on your level. They're not. Be wise enough to know that you're not better than anybody else, but know who you are. You have a higher calling, so continue to rise to the occasion and be who God has called you to be. You're not alone. There have been many before you who rose to the occasion and made their gifts and talents work for them. God isn't pleased with anybody who doesn't utilize what they have been given. Always keep in mind that there is a lot invested in you. You must make good on that return.

Never have a closed mind, but be optimistic about everything. Great pioneers never doubt. They understand just what it takes to accomplish their project, and they have the will to get it done.

You have a seed inside of you that you must nurture and cultivate to its full maturity. You don't have a choice in the matter. You will not rest until you are being the best version of yourself. God can't get glory out of someone's life if that person is not doing anything. It is action that makes one proud. It is action that separates you from the rest.

You will never look back on life and think, "I spent too much time with my ideas." Your real purpose in life is to develop yourself, how you carry yourself, and what you stand for. Everything that you accomplish is a part of your DNA. You can expect opposition, obstacles, and difficulties, but nothing can stop you from being who you were meant to be. As long as you have a desire to do more with your life, it will unfold. Maintain that positive energy and you will attract everything that you need for your success.

The world is unsettled. People have a false sense of pride. Everybody can be somebody on social media, but it's what you are doing in real life that's important. So let jokers joke and kids play. They are living unpurposeful lives, and they're in need of attention. People are not happy with themselves. They're depressed. You have a life because you have purpose in life. Stay about your business and strive for perfection.

Grind in secret and you will be rewarded openly. All the applause will come in return for the hard work and consistency that they don't see. It takes hard work and effort to become the best version of yourself.

Tell me: Do you really think everybody on social media is living their best lives? People can't stand to be by themselves because they will have to face their worst enemy. They would rather be in a relationship and make somebody else miserable instead of dealing with all the things that would make them complete. It's nobody else's responsibility to do for you what you must do for yourself. Nothing makes a person complete until they do all the things that they know they ought to be doing—businesswise, healthwise, familywise, and so on. Only you know what being the best version of yourself consists of. When you are that, you will find true inner peace.

When the warrior within you awakens, you will no longer procrastinate or make excuses for your life. You will do all that is necessary to stand up on your own two feet and be the person that you were built to be. We were not given the spirit of fear, but of courage and a sound mind. Believe in yourself and never doubt. Love is an action verb; it's not a word to just be thrown around. It's not a feeling or emotion; it's a cause for action. So when you say that you love yourself and yet you are not doing all the things that require action—that's not love.

Be real with yourself. Your mental health and emotional stability are most important when you are trying to accomplish anything. The mind controls the body, so take good care of it. Take care of your mind and it will take care of you.

You might lose some friends when you get serious about your life. If you do, they were never friends. Time is something that you can't get back, so separate yourself if need be and work on yourself. Misery loves company, so be mindful of that. You don't have time to waste. Be selective about whom you spend your time with. Wasted time is worse than wasted money. You can't get your time back, but money comes and goes. Life is made up of time, so if you love yourself and life, don't waste time.

There's nothing greater than inspiration. How you live your life is your expression of life. You will give others the courage to be the best that they can be. There's too much at stake. You can't put being great on hold for anything. It's not your destination that's important; it's your journey. If you want your children to excel in life, practice what you preach. Think big, trust yourself, and make things happen. Your children will do the same.

Do the universe a favor and don't hide your magic. Stay solid. Stay true to yourself and all that you do. Put your name on something. You have to be in it to win it. Your gifts that are lying dormant need to come alive. All those ideas that you used to have can still work for you, so stop procrastinating and get it together. As long as you have breath in your body, it's never too late. Your mental health is at stake because you will never have true peace of mind until you get it together.

Care enough for the people around you, and your family and friends will be inspired by that best version of you. It's all energy. We have the power to make others want to do better. That's powerful. Don't be selfish. Yes, it's easier to be negative than it is to be positive but nobody said that it would easy. There is dignity and honor behind every man's creation. Make a good impression with your God-given abilities. Use your mind and the rest will follow.

Nothing will ever happen for you unless you make it happen. Once you take the first step, a whole new world will open up for you. There are people and things waiting to align themselves with everything you're trying to accomplish, but you have to give the universe something to work with. All successful people know that they are successful before they ever accomplish anything. The confidence and the will to act upon what they believe in is inside them. They have the determination to work harder than most. They are perfectionists, and they make sure things get done. They're passionate and always optimistic. They believe that their futures can be brighter, and they use optimism as a strategy to accomplish those futures. They take responsibility for what could happen. They believe in all possibilities. Successful people are open-minded, making them very easy to connect with. They naturally make everybody feel important.

I choose to believe that everybody wants something. Deep down inside of you is a dream, and every now and then that dream floats to the surface of your conscious mind. You can either suppress it or give it life.

The reason people are depressed and not satisfied is because they are doing what they have to do to survive. They're not doing what they love doing. People are impressed by what society deems successful. They are trying to keep up. The workforce knows this. They have you sacrificing your dreams for money to survive. You're not living until you love what you're doing and can make a living doing it.

Your peace of mind is success. There is a war going on for the capture of your mind. Your time and energy are valuable. You were born to conquer and subdue, not to be used. Take a chance if you believe in yourself. It's not about impressing others but about living your life to its full potential.

Be true to who you are and don't be afraid to make mistakes. A life spent making mistakes is not only more honorable but more useful than a life spent doing nothing.

Most people lose because they can't see the win right in front of them. Have the courage to follow your heart and make your dreams a priority. Keep a positive attitude. Create your own opportunity—it is more empowering. Ultimately you only have one life to live, so make the best of it.

Life is full of distractions. Don't forget to be somebody. Take action and focus on what you want. Anything is possible once you set your mind to it. Turn your passion into success instead of spending your entire life somewhere you're passionless about.

There is no greater wealth in this world than peace of mind. Your mental health is wealth. If you're not content with the life you're living, it's time to create your own experiences and get excited about life.

Self-transformation is not about changing yourself. It means shifting yourself to a completely new dimension of experience and perception.

"If you don't know your own value, somebody will tell you your value, and it will be less than what you are worth." Love yourself enough to follow your dreams and do what is necessary to make those dreams happen. When you change your mind, things around you change. The biggest battles are always within. Don't conform but transcend. You have more power than you can imagine. "Therefore I say unto you, take no thought for your life, what ye shall eat, or drink; nor yet for your body, what you shall put on. Is not the life more than meat, and the body than raiment?"

People worry more about impressing other people than about being themselves. If someone asked you, "What is your purpose in life?" would you be able to tell them?

Life is more than just keeping up with the latest fashion. Life is more than cars, gold chains, and popping bottles. Life is not to be wasted. Life is about energy and productivity. Prosperity comes in many forms: soul, body, and mind.

There are an estimated ten thousand distinct religions worldwide. About 84 percent of the world's population is affiliated with Christianity, Islam, Hinduism, Buddhism, or some form of folk religion. People have a need to be better, to do better. They have a longing for a sense of higher self. God has said that he knew us before we were in the womb (Jer. 1:5). So you are really trying to get back to what you once were.

Spend time with yourself throughout each day to pray, meditate, or do whatever you do to connect with your higher self. I believe that it is everyone's first purpose in life to become a better person. It doesn't take religion to become the best version of yourself; it only takes self-awareness. We were born in a corrupt society, so you have to have the ability to unlearn and relearn. Don't be conformed to the world. Be transformed by the renewing of the mind. Evolve and move away from the crowd or you will end up like them.

Get into the habit of asking yourself, "Does this support the life I'm trying to create?" Your whole mindset has to change if you want to conquer. You must have the mind of a conqueror. Only the strong survive; the weak will be eaten alive.

Keep making progress in every area of your life. A little progress each day can add up to big results. Don't chase the world. It's temporary. Use the tool between your two ears to rise above madness and depression.

Be mindful of everything you take into your mind, body, and soul. Protect your spirit from negativity and create a peace that can't be disturbed. When you are positive and productive, you have no reason to be down or depressed. Unlearn the behaviors that hinder your growth as a person.

Once you change what's going on inside of you, you can change what's going on around you. Be committed to change, because without commitment, you will never start. Where there is work, there is progress. Nothing is accomplished on a bed of ease.

If you think a lot of money will make you happy, you've never had a lot of money before. Value your life, your children, and your goals. Money is a defense. It's good to have. But money is a promissory note for debt. No amount of money can bring you inner peace. Money is not the solution when you need to diet and exercise. Money is not the answer when you ought to stop drinking. Anybody can make money, but nobody can buy love for self.

Everyone knows just what it is that will bring them inner peace. Work on the things that will make you whole, entire, and complete before you chase money and material things.

Having a bigger house or a more fancy car than your neighbor doesn't make you a better person. How you treat yourself and others is what makes you a decent individual.

If you love yourself, do what is necessary and proper for you to be satisfied with yourself. Mental health is wealth. You can't accomplish anything when your mind isn't right. If you spend a lot of time inside your head, make sure it's a nice place to be.

It's nobody else's responsibility to make you happy. Nobody can decide how you ought to live. Nobody knows what's going on inside your head. They only know what you show them. When you think of doing something, you must act upon it. Plant a seed and give the universe something to work with. Whatever a person needs to do to be at peace with themselves, it starts with action.

Don't view life as a task instead an opportunity. You don't have to go to work. You have the opportunity to go to work and make some money. You don't have to lose weight. You have the opportunity to diet and exercise. You don't have to write that book or start a business—you have the opportunity to do so. It's about the journey of life and not the tasks.

Right now, today, you are someone's inspiration. So analyze life in a respectable frame of mind. If you can find something or someone worth dying for, you can find something or someone worth living for. Be passionate about something in life. If your job is stressing you, reconnect with your original goals. When you thought about going back to school or starting a business, what inspired you to think of this? Being a passionate person who knows what you want can bring excitement, joy, and a sense of true purpose to your life. Without passion, you only exist. Live out loud. You only have one life to live so why not make the best of it? Be the person that you know you're capable of being.

The lack of loyalty is one of the major causes of failure in every walk of life, so be true to yourself. Honor yourself by being the best version of yourself, and you will inspire others to do the same. You will feel complete, whole, and entire. You will lack nothing. The best is yet to come.

CHAPTER 7

LESSONS

I REMEMBER GROWING UP IN Flint, Michigan. We didn't always have what we wanted, but we always had what we needed. My dad was very conservative. He would cut my and my brother's hair, and at times, my mother would sew our clothes. When the ice cream truck would come on our block, we seldom got ice cream from it like other kids in the neighborhood. We didn't wear name-brand shoes such as Nike, Adidas, and Pumas. Dad wasn't about to spend that kind of money on some shoes. At that time, I thought it was because he had to provide for three children, my older brother, myself, and my younger sister. But it wasn't that he couldn't afford it because he always had good jobs. There was a lesson in everything. He worked for General Motors and was the manager at Toys R Us, the best jobs you could have back then. My dad was an entrepreneur. He graduated from Albany State University and later attended Mott Community College, where he graduated with a degree in business. He told me as I grew up, "I don't buy you Nike and all the name-brand clothes because I want you to understand that Nike is just a man. You can create your own clothing line if that's what you want to do. I don't buy you an ice cream from the ice cream truck all the time because you will enjoy it just for the moment. I prefer to buy you a box of ice cream, so you will enjoy it longer. Like the saying goes, "Give a man a fish, and he will eat for a day. Teach a man how to fish, and he will eat for a lifetime." That was hard to accept as a young boy, but I am so thankful for the lessons know that I'm older.

My dad put into action all that he taught us because he didn't work for someone else for too long. He opened his own business in downtown Flint, where he sold clothes, shoes, and accessories. He would always say, "You can have what the next man has." We would go out in the cold and pass out flyers advertising the business. He told me later in life if the internet was available at that time, he would have done things differently because he had to pay rent twice. He paid rent and lights on the business and the house.

Not only did my dad run his own business, my uncle, Eldredge Moss, ran a local barbershop. They came from a large family, seven boys and two girls. Most attended college, a couple enlisted in the army. Their parents believed in ownership. My grandparents owned their house, which is still in the family. All the brothers inherited land. Dad taught me to hold my head high and to carry myself with dignity. He said, "If I didn't have a dime in my pocket, I still looked like I was rich." He also taught me to always keep a pen and notepad so I won't forget my ideas. He taught me as a child about patent pending. At that time in life, I was into sports. During my early school years, I played basketball and football, and I wrestled. I never imagined that one day I would become a successful business owner. He taught me to ask questions. "There is no such thing as a dumb question," he reminded me, and I had plenty of questions to ask. I once asked him "Why do I see so many talented people who never make it?'" He replied, "There's such a thing as being afraid of success." I vowed then that anything I put my hands to I would take to the top. He always dressed professionally and carried a briefcase. At home he would sit at his desk in his office, doing paperwork. When we visited my uncle's home, I would sit among the grown-ups and hold conversations with them while the other kids played games in the basement.

Although I admired my dad growing up, it took a long time in life before business struck my interest. My brother and I would even stand in the showcase in the front of the store and pretend to be mannequins. Customers would walk by the window, and we would stand as still as possible. We drew much attention, and that was our purpose. My older brother always had me doing something crazy.

I knew that I was destined to be great. I always knew that I would do big things. I was told as a child that everything I touched turned into gold. My dad taught me as a child about buying wholesale. He would fly to New York and go to wholesale shops to purchase merchandise for the business. That's another reason he would not buy us expensive name-brand clothes; he was used to buying in bulk. He knew that it was the name on the shoes that made them expensive, not the material. "You can get that stuff cheap in New York," he would say. Business was like an extra class for me growing up. Math, science, social studies, PE, and business at home. "You can spend your whole life working for someone else, and when you die, they will replace you that same day." So, invest in yourself.

One day as a young boy I got caught stealing from a 7-Eleven. I put a Reese's Cup in my pocket. The cashier said, "I'm not going to call the police. I'm going to call your parents." I remember thinking, *Some favor.* I would have rather he called the police. To my surprise, when my dad came and picked me up, he bought me whatever I wanted. He said, "You don't have to steal. You can have anything you want. Remember that. Tell the man what you want, and speak louder." It was always a lesson in everything growing up. He raised me and my siblings according to our personalities. He never whooped me.

Now on the other hand, my mother was a different story. She didn't play the radio. I learned at an early age that I was somebody. We couldn't play with the other neighborhood kids' toys. We were taught to take care of our own things and to appreciate what we had. We were taught to hold our heads up high and be proud. My cousins were proud; they all were entrepreneurs. My older cousins were successful. My cousin Marty was on the cover of *Forbes* magazine. My cousin Ronnie now sings with The Spinners, and Bruce has an auto body shop in Atlanta and has done work for Snoop Dog.

Although I didn't have a clue as to what I wanted to be in life, from an early age I did know that I was destined for greatness. We had hobbies so after school we couldn't run to the streets after we finished our homework. My dad challenged us to find something that we liked to do. Work with our hands, sing, and dance. He really didn't care; just finding yourself was what was important. I wasn't good at anything but sports. I found my niche later in life, but we stayed doing our own things. We sold frozen cups, shoveled snow for money during the winter, and raked leaves during the fall. We had dance routines and would perform at house parties. We were thinkers as well as doers. We had chores and received an allowance. I'm not sure if kids these days know what that is. We learned what responsibility was and took pride in everything we did.

E. KINNARD MOSS

And I learned the importance of honesty. I returned to 7/11, and one day I had a chance to redeem myself after I got caught stealing. I came out of the store one day, and a gentleman dropped his wallet. I didn't think twice before returning to him. He was thankful, and it felt good to do a good deed. He reached in his wallet and gave me twenty dollars. I learned as a child that you could be rewarded for having integrity. It felt good to make someone else feel good. Now that I'm older, I understand that a good name is worth more than jewels. Things happen in your life when you are young to build character.

One day my dad came home and announced that he had found a house and a building for his new business in Birmingham, Alabama. We were about to move and leave our friends. This was me and my sister, Marcy's, first transition. My older brother had already moved to Georgia with our grandmother. My parents had sent him down South, where it was a slow-paced lifestyle. We didn't have any family in Birmingham. My sister and I thought that we were going to see cows and horses. We were from the North, and Birmingham sounded like the country.

To our surprise, some people were off the chain. These young gangsters were smoking cigarettes and marijuana and drinking alcohol. These cats were gangsters. I even felt the need to join a gang. It was just me and my sister, and I did whatever I had to do for us to be safe. I was fighting on the way to school and on the way home. Although I ran with a gang, it wasn't me; I knew I didn't come from that. I was smart enough to find a job at the age of twelve. I often felt that my life was in danger, so I needed something to do to rid the idle time. Every day after school I stopped at the convenience store and applied for a job. Of course, I was too young, but I refused to be turned down. The owner of the convenience store told me no several times, but I was persistent.

Finally, one day he said yes. I had gotten my first job, and I was so proud and excited.

Every day after school I would go to work. I started out washing windows, cleaning shelves, and sweeping and mopping the floor. My boss paid me twenty-five dollars a day. That was good, and I was only twelve years old. It wasn't long before I started working at the cash register. I felt really important then. I was envied by some of the guys in the neighborhood because I had a job and kept money in my pockets.

We only stayed in Birmingham for two years. My dad asked me if I wanted to stay or move to Georgia. I didn't want to leave because of the job. Besides, I was helping to pay the bills at home. My dad taught me responsibility at an early age, so he gave me the phone bill to pay. It was all good, but my life was in danger. I could have ended up dead or in jail. One of my closest friends at that time did end up going to prison, and another one was murdered.

(The richest soil is in the cemetery where dreams, lives, and ideas are buried.) EKinnard

Surely you weren't put on the earth to do nothing. Everyone has a purpose, and there is greatness inside all of us. You know your potential. When I was off course and running the streets, I was told that I would be dead by the time I was eighteen. Yet I knew that I was destined to be great. I never believed anything negative anyone ever said about me. I come from a respectable family. Strong people! Well-educated entrepreneurs who believe in ownership. My mother didn't have to work; my dad was the breadwinner. My mother planted flowers and took care of the home. My dad took us to professional baseball, basketball, and football games. We enjoyed amusement parks, and we traveled a lot. In retrospect, he must have been proud to be in a position to do this for his family. I speak highly of him because he taught us well. We learned what was important and what was not. He instilled in us not to spend our whole lives working for someone else and making them rich. They're just people, and if you use your minds, you can accomplish what the next person has accomplished.

CHAPTER 8

THE WORLD IS YOURS

ALL THINGS ARE POSSIBLE IF you are willing to commit yourself to what you believe in. We're all gifted and talented in our own ways. Anything worth having is worth working for. Once you put one foot in front of the other, you're on your way. Plenty of people have big dreams, but they don't know how to start. And if you don't know how to start, you're not going anywhere. Sometimes you have to go after what you want even though, your neither ready or sure. You will often surprise yourself if you just dare to be brave. When most people start out in business, they are never ready, but one thing leads to another. You must have the will to start. Failure is not an option. Life is short, and you can't put a date on your departure. So do great things while you have a chance, and let your work speak for you. If you do great things, your children are more likely to do great things. The world and everything in it is yours, but you must play your part. Don't let your life pass by. Be the best within yourself, no matter what you are trying to accomplish. Be more than just a dreamer. Work hard to accomplish your dreams and make them reality.

When you say this cannot be accomplished, and this cannot be done, you are shortchanging yourselves.

> My brain cannot process failure. It will not process failure. Because if I have to sit there and face myself and tell myself "You Are a Failure," I think that is almost worse than dying. (Kobe Bryant)

Kobe Bryant is a good example of how it's not how many years you live but the life in the years. Regardless of your situation, you must believe that you're somebody. You are greater than any mistakes that you have made. It's unfair to think that you can't accomplish what the next person has accomplished. Don't do that to yourself. Help yourself by being self-motivated. You will be an inspiration to others. There is nothing greater than to inspire others. Don't settle for less. There is greatness inside us all, but it's up to you to live your life to its full potential. What you want exists, so don't settle until you get it. True pleasure is when you can take pride in your accomplishments. All goals are reachable when you are focused. Stay in your own lane. It's easy to crash, but when you are in your own lane, you can drive backward if you like. Mind your business, and the world is yours. Go dormant if you must. Keep practicing, keep building, and one day you will shine. Successful people strive to be the best in every area of their lives. They are always looking for a way to become better people. Know your worth, and stay away from people who don't. Don't allow anything from your past to hold you back because your future needs you today.

Playing it safe isn't always good. We were born to make mistakes. Without mistakes there's no growth. That's how you learn and grow. Don't be too critical, but be willing to make mistakes; be willing to learn. Keep your head up to the sky. Never mind the small matters in life. Use those brain cells for your ambitions. Don't allow anything or anyone to stress you about anything. Mind your business, and you will excel. Life is for the living. Let the dead bury the dead. When something is not growing it just exists. Be productive. Love yourself and grow. The race is not given to the swift but to the ones who endure to the perfect end.

CHAPTER 9

ENERGY

EVERYTHING IS ENERGY. YOUR CONVERSATION is energy. You and I are made of energy. It's up to you to decide how to use it. Whatever energy you project into the world the universe will return an equal amount of that same energy back to you. You can choose to be positive or negative. It's all energy. No one was created for only one purpose. You have other work to finish, but you must focus on what is in front of you first. It only takes two good ideas to cause confusion in one's mind. Trying to focus on just one more thing will delay your process. Juggling a lot of things at once is fine if you're capable of doing so. The difference between being exhausted or vitalized depends on how you're mentally handling your tasks. It's all energy! Does your mind match your physical hustle? Your surroundings must be peaceful and supportive to accomplish a lot with little effort. You need positive energy to accomplish big things. Even when you are focused and driven, things can be overwhelming. It's up to the individual, but teamwork makes the dream become a reality. It's okay to do things for self-gratitude, but always have the mind to commend others. Be careful with your ego. There are enough people in this world with big egos.

As you help yourself, help others along the way. A body consists of many parts, but each part has its own function, performing together beautifully for the same cause. It's okay to need help as long as you're all working together for the same cause. Be appreciative. Your team must understand the vision and stay on the same accord. Don't over exhaust yourself. You just began, and you don't know it all. You're not there yet. Stay humble. Be willing to listen because constructive criticism is good when it's coming from a good place. There is always room to learn more and grow.

When it comes to business, you must have a tunnel vision and not care about what negative people may say or think. We all go through stages in life, and you must give everything to each stage. You will know that you have given your best when your efforts begin to bear fruits. "A good tree is known for its fruits." You cannot take too much to heart when you are trying to build a business. If you do so, you are not using your energy properly. Your conscience must agree with your subconscious in order to manifest what you're trying to accomplish. Your actions must continually be in one accord with your thoughts. You will know when you are channeling your energy in the right direction because you will outgrow most of your friends. Everything looks different when you are traveling in different directions.

Don't give up now. The energy you send out will come back to you, so only radiate the energy that you are willing to receive. Rely on yourself, and trust your hands. Be independent, and remember it's easy to do nothing, but where's the honor in that? How you use your energy will determine your outcome. The worst mistake that you can make is thinking that you have all the time in the world. You must stay consistent and be a doer. A vision without action is merely a dream.

Be diligent about your business. Either you plan to succeed, or you don't plan and fail. Consider the ant. The ants work all summer long preparing for the winter.

The world belongs to the energetic. (Emerson)

Invest your time and energy in building. Extraordinary people do extraordinary things. At the end of the day, take pleasure in your accomplishments. Grown-ups do grown-up things. I rise, I grind, and I shine. I use my mind and time wisely. Tomorrow is not promised to anyone, so whatever you set out to accomplish, stay focused and make it happen. Take an honest look at where you spend your time, energy, efforts, and emotions, and see where it is positively serving you. You were born to create and subdue the earth. If you want something badly enough, you will figure out a way to make it work for you. You can accomplish anything you want to accomplish. If the next person can do it, then so can you. You may have to work a nine-to-five job and spend two or three hours every day working on your business. It takes time. It takes energy. It takes a will and being consistent with your ideas to start a successful business. Put your energy and efforts toward the things that are beneficial for the improvement of your business and your life.

Be creative, and master your craft. It takes time and energy to make money. Use your money to advance, and always invest in your business ideas. The only way your situation will change is if you change it. I am a man of faith, but I am also a man of action. Before I started my business, I would pray so much I needed some kneepads. But one day God said, "Get up off your knees, and move on all that you have been praying for. Faith without action means nothing." The day that I began to pursue my dreams they became reality. I had thirty employees in thirty days.

The only thing that kept me from moving sooner was a lack of faith and the will to put one foot in front of the other. I had counted up the costs and couldn't see how I was going to pull it off. I was used to the normal, and what I wanted to accomplish wasn't normal. To me, that is. What made me push forward was knowing that I was born to do big things and refusing to settle. Don't wish for it; work for it. You can either spend your life trying to accomplish your dreams or help someone else establish theirs.

At some point everyone must focus on themselves, their ambitions, and their finances. You were born to be a leader, but don't expect anyone to follow you if you're not willing to give it your all. The generation after you will have its own ideas and goals. Will you be their inspiration? How will you persuade them to conquer their ambitions? Someone is always watching you. Your actions are important. I understand that I can have my own business and be successful because I watched my father do it. I work hard because I watched my father work hard. Spend time with yourself. Research and be willing to go the extra mile for what you want. The harder you work at something the better you will feel once you achieve it.

Business works for you when you have good intentions. My website has the testimonies of employees who speak highly of the company and the benefits of working from home. My intentions were to provide jobs for stay-at-home mothers and for people who have felonies on their records. I believe in reform and in second chances. With the advancement in technology, working from home is where it's at. I didn't just start a business for the money or to say that I have my own business. I started a business because I wanted to help people by introducing them to something new by providing job opportunities. It's very rewarding to hear people say that they prayed for such an opportunity. If your heart is good and you do your best, the money will come.

Have integrity. And in whatever business you set out to establish, treat people right so they will speak highly of you. Your business will flourish if you have pride and dignity about yourself. Word of mouth is still good advertising, so handle your business with care, and people will refer you to others as a good company with which to do business. A good name is worth more than emeralds and diamonds. You don't want t create a track record of doing bad business. People may not remember your name, but they will remember how they felt after doing business with you. People want to be able to trust you, and you have to be respectable. Don't treat people how you want to be treated. Treat them better. Go above and beyond to make sure you are doing your business with integrity and pride. When you do your best, people will brag about you to others, and you will create a good business name for your future.

Energy is everything, and if you use it right, you will see your business flourish. People who are successful in business don't spend their time with individuals who don't have the same mentality. It's lonely on your way to the top. You will outgrow your friends and family. You will be viewed differently from other people. Everybody can't go with you. You are a rare breed. Don't look down on people because most people are content with where they are in life. Your calling in life is not their call. I have missed weddings and funerals in order to stay focused on my business. Nobody will feel bad for you if you don't accomplish your goals. It's all up to you. These are your ideas and vision, so stay focused and mind your business.

You will be amazed at the things you can accomplish once you're focused. While your friends are watching football and drinking, you will be at home working on your dreams. "Energy is the key to creativity. Energy is the key to life. Your focus must remain sharp, and your time must be invested in your growth. Time is energy. Don't expect people to understand what you're up to. Stay positive, stay focused, and soon they will see. Energy is the strength and vitality required for sustained physical or mental activity. You can't afford to be concerned with small matters or everything that is going on in the world. It will drain your energy. Positive energy activates constant elevation. As long as you're doing something for the benefit of your business, it's progress. Keep putting positive energy into effect, and you will continue climbing.

Keep rising to the top, and be all that you can be. You can't expect people to believe in you or invest in your ideas. You must believe in yourself and find a way to make it work. When it's all said and done, you will feel better because you won't owe anyone anything. If you work hard and don't give up, you will feel the thrill of victory and not the agony of defeat. You have come this far because it's in you. So, continue to channel your energy in the right direction, and it will all unfold. Your energy is valuable and empowering. Use your energy wisely. Energy is everything, and everything is energy. Everything around us is energy, and you have the ability to control it with your thoughts. Think positive thoughts. What you think of yourself is what you will become. Keep rising to the top while your mind is telling you to give it all you got.

CHAPTER 10

THAT PART

DURING SLAVERY, THE SO-CALLED NEGRO here in America helped to build this country and never received reparations. They were left to pull themselves up by their bootstraps. It's a cruel joke to tell a bootless man to pull himself up by his own bootstraps. Eleven months before Dr. Martin Luther King Jr. was murdered, he began to talk about a new phase of the civil rights struggle. He spoke of the harsh reality of the so-called Negro that white Americans did not want to face. We were brought here in shackles against our will. When the slaves were freed in 1865 by the Emancipation Proclamation, we were given freedom and poverty at the same time, although there was a willingness to give other nations land and money to get started. America gave away millions of acres of land in the West and the Midwest. The so-called Negro was depersonalized and not considered a human being. This was justified on social, moral, and scientific levels in the eyes of white Americans.

Racism is still alive, and the color of one's skin is still a stigma. This is not to say that we have not come a long way because we're now able to do things that we once were not allowed to do. But for 240 years, free labor has truly been a white American legacy. Most so-called negroes won't receive an inheritance from their parents and It is farfetched to think that we will ever receive reparations. We must build our empires from scratch. We must do what is expected of us, and that is to pull ourselves up by way of education and information. We have truly had a hard life due to the racism that is yet still alive today. Our only way to overcome is to believe in your dreams. Work diligently with your hands. Network with like minded people. Research and obtain the information needed for progression.

Still I Rise
(Maya Angelou)

You may write me down in history
With your bitter, twisted lies,
You may trod me in the very dirt
But still, like dust, I'll rise.

Does my sassiness upset you?
Why are you beset with gloom?
'Cause I walk like I've got oil wells
Pumping in my living room.
Just like moons and like suns,
With the certainty of tides,
Just like hopes springing high,
Still I'll rise.

Did you want to see me broken?
Bowed head and lowered eyes?

Shoulders falling down like teardrops,
Weakened by my soulful cries?

Does my haughtiness offend you?
Don't you take it awful hard
'Cause I laugh like I've got gold mines
Diggin' in my own backyard.

You may shoot me with your words,
You may cut me with your eyes,
You may kill me with your hatefulness,
But still, like air, I'll rise.

Does my sexiness upset you?
Does it come as a surprise
That I dance like I've got diamonds
At the meeting of my thighs?

Out of the huts of history's shame juju
I rise
Up from a past that's rooted in pain
I rise
I'm a black ocean, leaping and wide,
Welling and swelling I bear in the tide.

Leaving behind nights of terror and fear
I rise
Into a daybreak that's wondrously clear
I rise
Bringing the gifts that my ancestors gave,
I am the dream and the hope of the slave.

I rise

I rise

I rise.

The Black Wall Street Massacre

Time plus injustice does not equal justice. In 1921 Greenwood, or Tulsa, Oklahoma, was a thriving, wealthy black community. It consisted of black doctors' offices, banks, beauty salons, grocery stores, movie theaters, and pharmacies. It was considered a golden age for downtown black-owned businesses. This story won't be found in most history books; it's one of the biggest cover-ups in history.

During this massacre, approximately one thousand black people lost their lives to racial violence. During a time when the KKK was alive and well, a young black teenager named Dick Rolland went into an elevator with a white girl named Sarah Page, who worked at the Drexel building. Something happened in the elevator. The white girl screamed, and Rolland came out running. Nobody knows what happened in the elevator, but a day later, Rolland was arrested and taken to the courthouse. Although Sarah refused to press charges the state picked it up. A large mob of angry whites gathered outside the courthouse, demanding justice. The local newspaper had hyped up the incident, saying that Rolland assaulted Page, although she did not press charges. It was a call to action for whites. The blacks of Tulsa came to the courthouse to protect Rolland. Someone in the angry mob had a gun. A black man asked him what he planned to do with the gun, and the angry man answered that he would use it. The black man attempted to disarm him, and the white man was shot. Hundreds of armed whites descended on what was called the black Wall Street.

Blacks went behind the railroad tracks that marked off the Greenwood district. The whites shot their way through. They looted, burned down buildings and homes, and murdered the productive citizens of the black Wall Street. More than twelve hundred homes were destroyed, and thirty-five blocks were burned down. A lot of records went missing from city files, and they were left to pick up the pieces. Some believe the US government played a role in the massacre. Some blacks in Tulsa testified to airplanes flying over Black Wall Street and dropping bombs. They described it as death from the sky.

Greenwood eventually rebuilt, but the part that haunts them to this day is that the bodies were never recovered. They were seen being hauled away in the back of trucks. They were once envied because of their wealth, but the blacks of Tulsa never received justice for the lives of their victims. Nor did they receive the insurance claims estimated at 2.7 million dollars.

The Chamber of Commerce in Tulsa has started a GoFundMe fundraiser to rebuild what was once a thriving, successful black community, built by blacks for blacks. The Greenwood district is seeking to raise $1 million in donations to rebuild the community that was destroyed by white supremacists in 1921. This is not just Tulsa's history; it's America's history. Freeman Culver is the president and chief executive officer of the Greenwood Chamber. During an interview with the *Tulsa World*, he brought up a very important conversation. He talked about how the money would not only help rebuild the buildings for black-owned businesses, it would preserve our history. It would show what we were capable of doing. "This is about remembering how resilient our people are." This is why we must never forget our history. This has been covered up for many years. To hide the injustice that was perpetrated on our people is also to hide the brilliance of our ancestors.

> A people without the knowledge of their past history, origin, and culture is like a tree without roots.
>
> (Marcus Garvey)

THE CONCLUSION OF THE MATTER

Weapons have formed against us and they have prospered against us, but they shall not prosper in the sense that we shall be utterly destroyed. This is the heritage of a spiritual people and a strong nation. We have faced many obstacles, but greater is the spirit of ambition that dwells within us. We are truly more than conquerors. We have the minds and wills to overcome every adversity we may face. How would you know that we're warriors if we never faced opposition? We're brilliant people capable of doing whatever we choose to do. Just like the city of Tulsa, Oklahoma, and black Wall Street. We have the minds to become doctors, lawyers, businessmen, and businesswomen. We will not focus on the hatred and injustice that were perpetrated on our people, but we must never forget.

Today we face some of the same injustices, but our history shows you just who we are and what we're capable of doing and overcoming. We will not give the enemy power over our souls and make us hate. We must encourage our brothers and sisters to be the best they can be. We are the light of the world, and it's time to bring forth our light from behind the bush and the darkness of our past. Accomplish what you set out to do regardless of adversity. Accomplish what you have set out to do through all the heartache and pain. We're truly warriors, so recognize your strengths, because you have all the potential in the world. Be productive!

ABOUT THE AUTHOR

Ekinnard Moss is the founder of Emerald Enterprise Corporation and author of There's A Good Brother Right Around The Corner and Striving 4 Perfection. Through his mentorship and leadership, he has provided jobs to many across the US as well as encouragement to youth and others to believe there is greatness inside each of them. Moss is a motivational speaker and a proud father of four who lives in Orlando, Florida.

Printed in the United States
by Baker & Taylor Publisher Services